Opposites Attract:
Magnetism

Steve Parker

Heinemann
LIBRARY

www.heinemann.co.uk/library
Visit our website to find out more information about **Heinemann Library** books.

To order:

 Phone 44 (0) 1865 888066

 Send a fax to 44 (0) 1865 314091

 Visit the Heinemann Bookshop at www.heinemann.co.uk/library to browse our catalogue and order online.

First published in Great Britain by Heinemann Library, Halley Court, Jordan Hill, Oxford OX2 8EJ, part of Harcourt Education Ltd.
Heinemann is a registered trademark of Harcourt Education Ltd.

Editorial: Sarah Eason and Kathy Peltan
Design: Jo Malivoire/Ascenders
Picture Research: Ruth Blair and Debra Weatherley
Production: Edward Moore

Originated by Ambassador Litho Ltd.
Printed and bound in Hong Kong and China by South China Printing Company Ltd.

The paper used to print this book came from sustainable resources.

ISBN 0 431 16741 9
08 07 06 05 04
10 9 8 7 6 5 4 3 2 1

British Library Cataloguing in Publication Data
Parker, Steve
Opposites Attract: Magnetism. – (Everyday Science)
538
A full catalogue record for this book is available from the British Library.

Acknowledgements
The publishers would like to thank the following for permission to reproduce photographs: Alamy/Goodshoot p.5; Corbis pp.22, 44; Corbis/Noboru p.16, Corbis/Bettman p.19 Drew Super Photography/Photographersdirect.com p.6; FLPA/Minden Pictures/Mike Parry p.26; Fraser Photos pp.4, 33; Getty p.52; Getty/BrandX Pictures p.30; Harcourt Education p.7; Harcourt Index p.51; High Field Magnet Laboratory, University of Nijmegen, the Netherlands p.50; Robert Harding p.23, Robert Harding/Brouard p.35; SPL p.48, SPL p.8/ Megna, SPL/Tek Image p.9, SPL/Volker Steger p.13, SPL/Professor Brian Wilshire p.14, SPL/Bluestone p.15, SPL/ Sinclair Stammers p.18, SPL/NASA p.27, SPL/Bartel p.28, SPL/Stock p.36, SPL/Siu p.42, SPL/Nunuk p.46, SPL/Tompkinson p.49; Trip p.45 Tzaud Photo/ Photographersdirect.com p. 17.

Cover photograph of the *aurora borealis* reproduced by permission of Robert Harding.

Artwork: Art Construction pp.13, 47; Ascenders p.34; Mark Franklin pp.20, 25, 29, 39, 40, 43; Visual Image p.11.

The publishers would like to thank Robert Snedden for his assistance in the preparation of this book.

Contents

Words appearing in bold, **like this**, are explained in the Glossary.

Mysterious magnetism

Magnets are strange. In everyday life they can be note-holders that clamp bits of paper to the fridge or pin-holders to gather paper clips and sewing needles or cupboard latches that keep doors closed.

Picky stickers

Magnets are mysterious because they only work on some substances. A magnet is usually a small lump of metal that seems to grab certain items and stick to them with an invisible strength. Yet a magnet has no effect at all on other substances, such as wool, paper, wood or glass.

Sticky spelling
Many of us encountered magnets when we learned to read and spell, in the form of magnetized letters that can be stuck to metal surfaces. Although 'sticky' they can be moved easily.

An unseen force

Magnets are also mysterious because their **force** is invisible. The **magnetic force** or magnetism spreads out from a magnet, usually into the air, without showing itself. Sometimes we hold or move something near a magnet and it is grabbed as if by an unseen hand – this is magnetism at work. Magnetism works not only in air, but also under water, and even in the emptiness of a vacuum where there is no air or anything else. Strong magnetism can also pass through thin layers of substances like paper, card, glass or cloth. So, a magnet on one side of a sheet of card can attract an object on the other side.

Magnetism is also difficult to understand. Usually it is explained in terms of the tiny particles, called **atoms,** that make up all objects and substances in the Universe. The explanations of how magnetism works can get very technical. This is partly because scientists still do not fully understand the nature of magnets and how they exert their invisible forces. Also, the explanations are quite similar to the explanations of something else we use every day – electricity. Even in modern science, magnetism and electricity are sometimes confused.

Magnetism and history

Over 2500 years ago, people in Ancient Greece knew how a particular kind of rock, lodestone, would pull certain other kinds of rock towards it. In some cases, if the other rock was another lump of lodestone, the two pieces would repel each other. Lodestone, today also called magnetite, is now known to be a mineral with natural magnetism. Since those ancient times, magnetism has fascinated and puzzled people and been a challenge for scientists to explain.

Magnetism says 'it's me'

A cash or credit card has a strip of magnetic particles which contains information about the owner. If the information does not match the security number entered by pressing the keys, the card does not work.

Magnetism and us

In modern life, magnetism is used far more widely, and in applications with much more practical value than fridge note-holders. It is essential for the workings of thousands of machines and gadgets from televisions, computers and mobile phones, to microwave ovens, cars and medical scanners. Any equipment with an electric **motor**, from a bullet train to an electric toothbrush, uses magnetism.

Besides this, magnets and magnetism are important away from daily life, for instance out in space, or for exploring remote lands, or watching the vast shimmering curtains of light in the night sky near the North and South Poles. Magnets may be strange and mysterious, but they are very widespread and very useful – in fact, they are essential in our modern world.

Simple but useful

Magnets are rarely obvious, and this is especially true of **permanent magnets** in daily life. They are so unnoticed we rarely realize we are using them. They perform their tasks silently. Yet they are almost everywhere. In addition to the uses of permanent magnets described below, can you think of any others?

Everyday magnets
Many screwdrivers are also magnets, so they helpfully hold on to steel screws or lift them from holes.

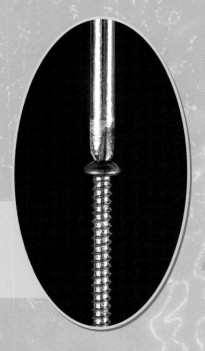

Destroying magnetism

Most permanent magnets keep their magnetic force for many years, but not for ever. The force fades with time and use. Knocking a magnet hard several times can cause its magnetism to disappear straight away. If a permanent magnet is heated above a certain **temperature**, it loses its magnetism completely. The exact temperature at which this occurs varies depending on which materials were used to make the magnet, and is called the Curie temperature, after French scientist Pierre Curie (1859–1906). For a typical everyday magnet made of iron-based steel, the Curie temperature is about 750–800 °C.

Tools and utensils

Knives are sharp and dangerous, and should be stored safely, especially in the kitchen. A magnetic knife-holder has a long, strip-like magnet that attracts the steel blades of knives, to keep them securely out of the way. Magnetic door catches and closers on cupboards and fridges work in the same way.

When you open a food can, the cut edge of the lid can also be dangerous. Many hand-powered and electrical can-openers include a magnet that attracts the steel of the lid as it comes away from the rest of the can, and holds it safely out of the way for careful disposal.

Steel-based pins, needles, nails and screws have sharp points and can also cut us. If they are spilled on the floor, you can use a magnet to pick them up safely. If they fall down a crack or somewhere awkward, a magnet on a string or bar can lift them out. Screwdrivers also have magnetic tips for gripping the screws.

The abilities of magnetism to pass through a thin layer of some substances, and to work in water, come in handy when cleaning windows. A strong magnet is placed on one side of the glass. It attracts a metal layer inside the sponge or cloth on the other side of the glass. As the magnet is moved about, the sponge or cloth on the other side 'follows' it and is pulled along the surface, wiping the glass clean. Magnetic cleaners like this are useful for places where people cannot reach, such as the outside of large windows in a high building.

Hold on tight
In 'travel chess' the pieces have small magnets in their bases. These hold them on to the metal board so they do not fall over in unsteady places like cars, trains and buses.

Toys and games

Magnets are used in many toys and other products used for fun, because of their 'stickiness'. Plastic letters, numbers and shapes can have small magnets on the back, so they can be stuck to a magnetic board or to an appliance such as a fridge. Some toy trains use magnets to join their carriages. Fishing games use magnets on strings to catch the metal fish in a pretend pool. Sports games use magnets on sticks, which are put under the pitch to attract the magnetic bases of the players.

Features of a magnet

Perhaps the most familiar type of magnet is the bar magnet. It is often shaped like a bar or rod, but a magnet can also be a square block, rounded disc, ring, ball or a horseshoe. This familiar kind of magnet is called a permanent magnet, because its magnetic force is always present.

All shapes and sizes
Permanent magnets come in many designs and sizes, attracting each other and also steel objects, such as paper clips.

Attracted by a magnet

The standard bar magnet shows the basic features of any permanent magnet. It attracts or pulls certain objects, and they stick to it. An object that is attracted by a magnet is said to be magnetic. Many common substances, such as plastic, glass, paper, wood, wool and pottery are not magnetic. The most common magnetic substance is the metal iron. However, iron is rarely used in its pure form to make everyday objects. Usually it has carbon added to it. Between them these two elements are used to make the metallic alloy called steel (or carbon steel), which is very common in daily life.

Hard and soft magnetic materials

Permanent magnets made of steel are usually **hard**. This does not indicate their physical hardness, but how long they retain their magnetism. Magnets are made by putting a piece of iron or steel into the very powerful force of another magnet. When the other magnetic force is taken away, then if the magnetism remains, the substance is called hard. If the magnetism fades quickly, it is called **soft**. Hard magnets, which are the familiar permanent magnets, are usually made of steel. Soft magnets are usually made of iron and they have many uses in **electromagnets**, electric motors and electrical **generators**, as we will see in this book.

Farther = weaker

The strength of a magnet's force does not fade in a regular way with increasing distance from the magnet. It becomes much weaker, very quickly. If you double the distance from the magnet, you do not decrease the force by half, but by 8 times. If you triple the distance, the force decreases 27 times. Scientists call this the cube rule. 2 cubed, or $2 \times 2 \times 2 = 8$; and 3 cubed, or $3 \times 3 \times 3 = 27$. This is why the pull of a magnet on a magnetic object does not seem very strong until the object is right next to it.

Two poles

Another feature of a magnet is that its magnetic force is strongest at two places called **poles**. On a bar magnet, there is a pole at each end. We can feel this when the bar magnet attracts a magnetic item such as a paper clip. The clip is held most strongly at one pole. A horseshoe magnet is like a bar magnet bent around into a U shape, so its poles are closer together. This combines their magnetic force into a smaller area, so a suitably-sized item can be held more strongly, with two poles instead of one. On a disc-shaped magnet there is usually a pole on each of the flat sides. As explained later, the two poles are not the same. They are usually called north or positive, and south or negative.

Polar attraction

Magnetism is strongest at a magnet's poles. The poles are at the ends of this horseshoe magnet, so tiny pieces of iron filings stick mainly here.

What is magnetism?

It is fairly easy to describe what a magnet looks like and what it does. But why does a magnet have the special power of attracting certain objects, mainly those containing iron? The answer lies in the particles, called **atoms**, which make up all substances and all matter. Everything is made of atoms, but they are far too small to see. The blob of ink that forms the dot on this 'i' contains more than ten billion atoms.

Why iron?

The lining up of tiny magnetic domains cannot happen in just any substance. Each kind of pure substance or chemical element, such as iron or carbon or aluminium, has its own type of atom, with a unique number of electrons and other subatomic particles. Iron has 26 electrons and this number, along with the pattern of the orbits and spins of the electrons, is best at producing a magnetic force. Iron-containing metals are also known as **ferrous metals**, and so the ordinary type of magnetism, which attracts them, is called ferromagnetism.

Inside the atom

Atoms may be very, very small – but they are not the smallest things. Each atom is made of even tinier parts, called **subatomic particles**. There are three main kinds of subatomic particle – **protons**, **neutrons** and **electrons**.

Protons and neutrons are at the centre of an atom, grouped closely together into a bunch known as the **nucleus**. Electrons are much smaller and lighter and they are outside the nucleus. They can be imagined as moving around the nucleus, almost like satellites orbiting planet Earth. The protons in all kinds of atoms are the same. So are the neutrons, and so are the electrons. What makes the difference between atoms of one substance, such as iron, and another, such as copper, is the numbers of these particles in each atom. Some atoms have just a few subatomic particles, while others have more than 200. Iron, the main magnetic substance, has 26 protons, 30 neutrons and 26 electrons.

As the electrons move around the nucleus, they also spin around – like the Earth, which turns like a top as it orbits the Sun. Electrons have a type of energy or charge called **electric charge**. As they spin and orbit, their moving electric charges make a magnetic force, which we will investigate further later. The charge of an electron is termed negative. The charge of a proton is known as positive. In most atoms, the number of electrons is equal to the number of protons. So the two kinds of charge balance each other, and the atom as a whole is neither positive nor negative.

All lined up

However, moving charges make a magnetic force. So each atom, with its spinning, orbiting electrons, is like a tiny magnet with its own magnetic force due to these moving electrons. It has regions of greatest magnetic force, like two poles. In most substances, the magnetic forces of individual atoms do not line up. They face in various directions at random. So the billions of atoms in an object all have magnetic forces working in different directions, and they cancel each other out. There is no overall magnetic force. In a magnet, the magnetic forces of the atoms are all lined up, or aligned. They all face the same way. Their magnetism combines into larger areas called **domains**, which are like tiny bar magnets. The domains in turn combine to form the magnetic force of the whole magnet.

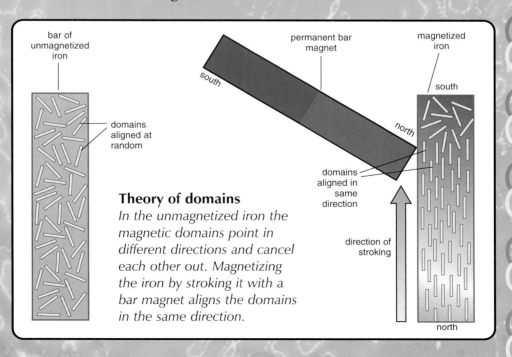

bar of unmagnetized iron

permanent bar magnet

magnetized iron

south

south

north

domains aligned at random

domains aligned in same direction

Theory of domains

In the unmagnetized iron the magnetic domains point in different directions and cancel each other out. Magnetizing the iron by stroking it with a bar magnet aligns the domains in the same direction.

direction of stroking

north

The magnetic field

We can see the effects of **magnetic force**, when a magnet attracts an object containing iron. We cannot, however, see the **force** itself.

We can draw a diagram of the invisible magnetic force, which helps to explain where it is and what it does. The original idea for this came from English scientist Michael Faraday, in the 1830s. Faraday did many experiments investigating magnetism and electricity. He also made early versions of many electrical–magnetic devices, such as the electric **motor** and electrical **transformer**.

The greatest experimenter

English scientist Michael Faraday (1791–1867) worked on electricity, magnetism, chemicals, forces and many other areas of science. He was one of the greatest-ever experts at building equipment and conducting experiments. From the 1830s he studied the links between electricity and magnetism. Faraday became famous at the Royal Institution in London, and the Christmas Faraday lectures are still held there in his honour.

A field of magnetism

The region around a magnet where the magnetic force is present is called the **magnetic field**. The size of the magnetic field varies according to the size and the strength of the magnet. The magnetic field of a small but very powerful magnet may extend farther than that of a larger but weaker one. The magnetic field does not suddenly stop at a certain distance from the magnet. It fades away with distance, as we have seen. For example, the magnetic fields of everyday small bar magnets, such as those which hold paper notes to the fridge, extend outwards about five to eight centimetres. Further than a certain distance from the magnet, however, the field is so weak and ineffective that for practical purposes we can imagine it as zero.

Magnetic objects

When a piece of iron is placed in a magnetic field, the field makes the piece of iron into a magnet itself, by making its **domains** line up. This is known as **magnetic induction**. The piece of iron pulls on the real magnet, which pulls back. This is why an iron object is magnetic, or attracted to a magnet. As soon as the magnetic field is taken away, the domains of the piece of iron become jumbled again, and so it is no longer a magnet.

Magnetic field

Near the poles the lines of magnetic force are closest, showing that the field is strongest there. Between the poles the lines spread out to show that the field is weaker.

lines of magnetic force

south pole

north pole

Lines of force

A magnetic field is often drawn in a diagram by using lines that run from one **pole** of the magnet to the other. This is a useful idea, because the lines show that the magnetic field has a direction, from one pole to the other. It is also useful because a stronger magnetic field can be shown by making the lines closer together.

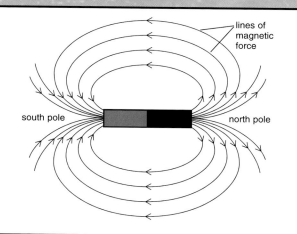

Measuring magnetism

The overall strength of a magnetic field, known as **magnetic flux**, is measured in units called **webers**. The number of webers shows the total force of the whole magnetic field around a magnet (see page 52). Another way to measure magnetism is in **teslas**. As we will see later, this shows the closeness of the lines of force in a particular part of the field.

Measuring electromagnetism
The magnetic field of the motor in an electric drill is measured, to see how it will stand up to knocks and wear and tear after it has been well used.

Not just iron

Iron is the main substance involved in magnetism. But other metals and materials are magnetic and can be made into magnets, too. One such substance is nickel, a very hard and shiny metal, used to make 'silver' coins. Another is cobalt, another hard metal, used in machine parts that have to be very tough. Rarer materials that are magnetic are neodymium, gadolinium and dysprosium. These belong to a group of substances called rare earth metals or rare earths, because they were once thought to be rare in the Earth's rocks. In fact we now know that some of them are more plentiful that many other metals.

Mixed magnets

Many of the permanent magnets in daily use, around the home and in machines, are made of mixtures of various metals and other substances. These mixtures or blends are called alloys. The various kinds of steel are alloys of iron, blended with carbon and usually additional metals. Scientists have spent many years testing various metals and alloys to see if they can make stronger magnetic materials. It is not only the strength of the magnet that is important, but also whether the magnetic material is tough and long-lasting, can resist knocks or vibrations, and will keep its magnetism for a long time.

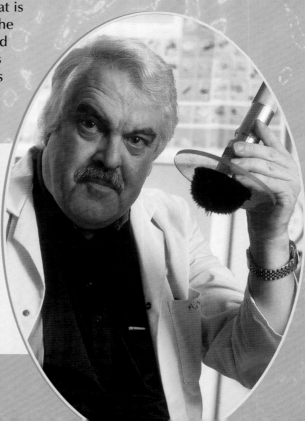

No hiding place
A new type of magnetic fingerprint powder may give clearer prints more quickly than the traditional type, for use in police investigations. The inventor of this new method is British scientist Professor Brian Wilshire.

Small, light sounds

Headphones have two large cup-like parts, one to fit over each ear. Inside each cup is a small version of a loudspeaker, with a powerful magnet. In the 1960s scientists testing new magnetic materials invented samco, or samarium-cobalt. Permanent magnets made from it were small and light, yet very powerful. This allowed the development of earphones, where the magnet and whole speaker-like device could be made small enough to wedge into the ear.

Tiny magnets
Each earphone has a tiny magnet within a plastic case that can fit into the ear.

Types of magnetic material

In general, everyday types of permanent magnet are made from two groups of materials – non-rare earth and rare earth. The non-rare earth materials include alnicos and ceramics. Alnico (Al-Ni-Co) permanent magnets are a combination of the metals aluminium, nickel and cobalt. They are not expensive to make, but they tend to lose their magnetism more easily than other types. Ceramic permanent magnets, also called **hard** ferrites, contain iron in the form of iron oxide, and also the substances strontium and barium. They can be cheap to make and powerful, but they are also very brittle so they crack or splinter easily.

More power

The rare earth magnetic materials include samco or samarium-cobalt (Sm-Co), and neodymium-iron-boron (Nd-Fe-B). Magnets made from them tend to be expensive, but they have great power for their size. The ability of a substance to retain its magnetic field over a long period is called **retentivity**. The steel alloys used to make permanent magnets have high retentivity. They need a very strong magnetic field to make them magnetic, but when that field is taken away they keep their magnetism very well for a long time.

Attract and repel

If a magnet is put near a magnetic substance, the magnet attracts it. But what happens if a magnet is put near another magnet? One of two things. The two magnets may pull powerfully towards each other, or they may repel each other, also very strongly. This happens because the two poles of a magnet are not the same, they are opposite to each other. One pole is called the positive, + or north pole. The other is known as the negative, – or south pole. The names north and south were used by French scientist Peter Peregrinus in about 1280. At this time magnets were becoming more common in the form of devices called magnetic compasses, used by sailors to find their way at sea.

Maglev

The pushing force between the like poles of two magnets, or the pulling force between unlike poles, can be strong enough to lift many people – and the train carriage they are in. These types of train are **maglevs**, which is short for magnetic levitation. It means lifting or levitating an object so that it appears to float, using magnetic forces. In one system, magnets in the train repel magnets in the track and the train levitates above the track. Maglevs are used in a few small-scale railway-type systems, mostly in city centres and at airports. They do away with noise, vibration and wear of wheels. But they need a lot of electrical energy to make the magnetic fields, because they use **electromagnets** (see page 28).

Japanese maglev train
Maglev trains give a smooth, quiet ride but they need huge amounts of electricity to charge their electromagnets.

Like and unlike

Peregrinus found that if the north pole of one magnet is held near the north pole of another magnet, the two poles repel each other. If two south poles are put near each other, they also repel each other. If a south pole and a north pole are brought near to each other, however, they attract each other. Peregrinus first came up with the rule we use today: 'Like poles repel, unlike poles attract.' This is vitally important, not only in the study of magnetism but in using electricity and in many other areas of everyday science. A similar principle is used in electricity, where the same electric charges (such as two positives) repel, but positive and negative attract.

Magnetic induction

As described earlier, when a permanent magnet attracts a magnetic object, it causes or induces the object to become a magnet. This is only temporary though. If the object is stuck to the magnet's north pole, the part of the object next to the north pole will temporarily become a south pole. The farthest part becomes a temporary north pole.

Then, if another magnetic object is brought near, the temporary or induced magnet will attract it, too and so on. This is how a powerful magnet can pick up a whole chain of small objects such as paper clips or pins, as each one becomes a small temporary magnet. The magnetism becomes weaker at each link along the chain. If the clip closest to the permanent magnet is pulled off, the magnetism along the chain disappears and the chain falls apart.

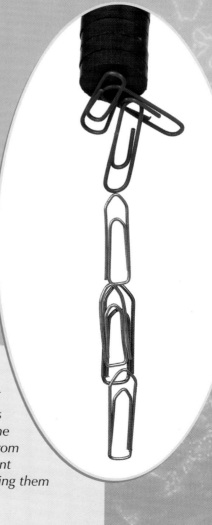

Magnetic induction
This string of paper clips is passing on the magnetism from the permanent magnet holding them in line.

Magnetism and electricity

Today we know that magnetism and electricity are related. In fact they are parts of the same general force, electromagnetism. For hundreds of years, though, people either thought that they were the same thing – or that they were completely different.

Lodestone (magnetite)
This naturally magnetic rock was known in ancient times in Magnesia, now part of northern Greece.

The power to pull

It was known in Ancient Greece that substances such as amber could be given powers of attraction. Amber is the golden-coloured resin or juice of ancient trees, preserved and hardened over millions of years. If a piece of amber was rubbed briskly with a cloth, it would attract lightweight objects such as feathers. Today this is explained as being due to electrostatic charge, or **static electricity**. It is the same force that makes a blown-up balloon stick to the wall after it has been rubbed on clothing.

Different but the same

In the 1600s and 1700s scientists carried out more experiments and began to find some of the differences between magnetism and electricity.

Why magnet?

The term 'magnet' may come from the name of a region in Greece called Magnesia. This was part of Thessaly, which is now an area of northern Greece. The rock lodestone (magnetite), which has natural magnetism, was well known there. It lay on the ground looking like other stones and people were fascinated by its property of attraction.

In the 1820s, Hans Christian Oersted and André-Marie Ampère discovered very close links between magnetism and electricity, and how one could generate the other. In the 1870s, Scottish scientist James Clerk Maxwell explained mathematically how magnetism and electricity were both part of the same basic force, electromagnetism.

Magnetic and electric

A fire gives out light for us to see by. It also gives out heat to keep us warm. The fire is the same in both cases, but it can be described in two different ways, as bright or hot. Likewise, magnetism and electricity are two views of the same force, and one accompanies the other. Together they are called electromagnetism.

The **electromagnetic force** is found everywhere: within atoms, in our machines and gadgets, all around our planet Earth, even across the entire Universe. It is one of the most basic or fundamental forces known to science. However, the confusion between magnetism and electricity continued for a long time. In the year 1600, English scientist William Gilbert wrote a book about his experiments both with magnets, and with what we now call static electricity. He named his book *De Magnete* or 'About Magnets'. Perhaps this was not surprising, because the word 'electricity' was almost unknown at the time. It had just been invented – by William Gilbert.

Great Englishman

William Gilbert (1544–1603) worked in many areas of science, but foremost he was a doctor – England's royal physician for Elizabeth I and James I. Away from his patients, Gilbert was fascinated by magnetism. He studied how an iron object could be made into a magnet by stroking it with another magnet, and how heating a magnet made its magnetism disappear. He helped to establish that the Earth was like a giant magnet. His book, *De Magnete* (1600), was read by famous scientists across Europe. It is often called the first great English scientific work.

William Gilbert
William Gilbert was a brilliant researcher of magnetism.

Magnetic Earth

What is the biggest magnet you have ever seen? Look around and outside, and you will see it – the Earth. Our whole planet is a magnet. It was William Gilbert who first realized this, more than 400 years ago. Even so, Gilbert did not know how Earth makes its magnetism. Today the reason is clearer. The occurrence of the **magnetic force** is due to the inner structure of the planet.

Deep in the Earth

Planet Earth is a giant ball about 12,700 kilometres (7900 miles) across. The outer layer of solid rock, the crust, is very thin. Below is a much thicker layer of part-melted rock, the mantle.

At the planet's centre is a huge round blob, the core, of iron and nickel at tremendous pressure and temperature – more than 3000 °C. As the Earth spins, parts of the core flow slowly like thick treacle. The swirling motion of the iron makes electrical currents which then produce magnetism, as explained on later pages.

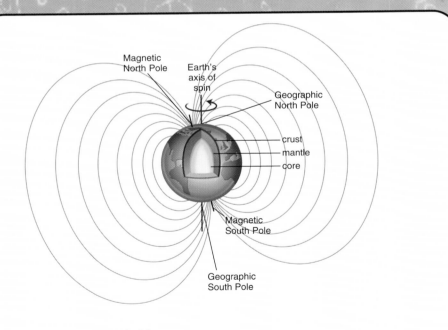

Magnetic North Pole

Earth's axis of spin

Geographic North Pole

crust
mantle
core

Magnetic South Pole

Geographic South Pole

Earth's magnetic field
The magnetic lines of force curve from one magnetic pole to the other. These magnetic poles are some distance from the Geographic North and South Poles.

Earth's magnetic field

The Earth's **magnetic field** has been mapped and measured in detail. The lines of magnetic force run from the top or northern end of the Earth, around and down to the southern end. The place at each end where we can imagine all the lines of force coming together at their strongest, and heading down into the ground, is called the magnetic **pole**. The one in the northern region or Arctic is the Magnetic North Pole, and the one at the opposite end, in the Antarctic, is the Magnetic South Pole. These places and their importance are described further on the next page. Earth's magnetic field is not just on the surface. It is inside the planet, and also extends far above it, up through the air and out into space.

Earth is not the only planet that has magnetism. Other planets in space do, and so do the Sun, other stars and many other giant objects deep in space. Magnetism is present all across the Universe.

How strong is Earth's magnetism?

The strength of a magnetic field within a certain area can be imagined as the closeness of its lines of **force** (as shown in the diagram opposite). The scientific name for this strength is **magnetic flux** density, measured in **teslas**. At a certain place on the planet's surface – say Washington, DC, USA – the Earth's magnetic field is 0.000057 teslas. The small **permanent magnets** in earphones are more than 1000 times more powerful. (One tesla is equal to one **weber** per square metre.)

A varied field

Earth's magnetic field is not equally strong everywhere. It varies slightly, for a number of reasons. One is the amount of iron in the rocks. Rocks with a lot of iron tend to affect the Earth's lines of magnetic force. Very sensitive devices, called magnetometers, can measure these variations in magnetism. They help prospectors and surveyors find new sources of useful rocks and minerals.

Magnetism underwater
Divers use magnetometers to map Earth's magnetism at various depths of water through the oceans.

Finding the way

Earth's natural magnetic field can be used in many ways. One of the commonest is finding directions or navigating. The main device for doing this is the magnetic compass or navigational compass. For hundreds of years people used magnetic compasses, without really understanding how they worked, to find their way across sea and land.

Age of discovery

Compasses were in use in ancient China about 2200 years ago, and possibly well before this time. Those early compasses were made from the naturally magnetic rock called lodestone. From about the 1100s, compasses were used on ships to navigate across oceans, first by sailors from China, then in East Asia. By the 1300s, Europeans were using them too. Magnetic compasses helped to open the way for the Age of Discovery, during the fifteenth to seventeenth centuries, when sailors explored distant parts and travelled all around the world.

A typical compass

A standard magnetic compass consists of a long, thin magnet, the needle. It is free to swing around or pivot, usually on a sharp point near its middle. Each end or pole of the compass needle attracts the unlike pole of another magnet – the Earth. The compass swings around so one end points to the Earth's Magnetic North Pole and the other end to the Magnetic South Pole.

Magnetic compass
A compass must be held level so the needle can turn easily to show north. Then the map will be held in the correct position to find the route.

Compass on board

On a ship, the compass floats in a bowl or bath of oil, so that it remains level and steady as the ship itself tilts in the waves. Back on dry land, compasses are also useful for everyday tasks, such as making sure a television aerial or dish points in the correct direction to receive the best signals.

Two norths and two souths?

The True or Geographic North and South Poles are the places around which the Earth spins. The Earth rotates on an imaginary line, its axis, every 24 hours. The Geographic North and South Poles are the ends of this axis. But a compass points to the Magnetic North and South Poles. These are where the lines of magnetic force are strongest. They are in different places from the Geographic Poles, owing to the way Earth's magnetism is made deep in its core. Detailed maps are marked with directions for both the True and Magnetic Poles.

The Magnetic North Pole is near Bathurst Island in northern Canada, about 1300 kilometres (810 miles) from the True North Pole.

The Magnetic South Pole is in the sea off the coast of Wilkes Land, about 2800 kilometres (1740 miles) from the True South Pole on Antarctica itself.

Wanderings, dips and flips

A magnetic compass needle does not always point directly at the North Magnetic Pole. Due to small-scale local changes in Earth's magnetic field, it may point a few degrees to the west (left, facing north) or east (right, facing north). These slight variations are due partly to how much iron the rocks in the area contain. High levels of iron in a rock tend to bend the lines of force into the rock, away from other rocks nearby which contain less iron. The difference in angle between the direction of the compass needle and the true direction of the North Magnetic Pole, is called the angle of **declination**. It is marked on the very accurate maps used by sailors, pilots, explorers, surveyors, space scientists and others, so they can take it into account.

Still important

For many everyday uses, when navigating and finding the way, the magnetic compass has been replaced by the Global Positioning System (GPS). This is a series of satellites in space that beam radio signals down to receivers on Earth. Using a GPS receiver, a person can find True North, and his or her position to the nearest 30 metres or less. However, GPS receivers sometimes break down, run out of battery power or fail to detect the satellite signals. So people who travel in remote places or navigate craft still learn to use a magnetic compass.

The angle of dip

At the Magnetic North and South Poles, the lines of magnetic force go straight into the ground. As you travel away from either pole, the angle at which the lines enter the ground becomes lower. This angle at which the lines enter the ground is called **inclination**, or dip. It varies from 90° at the Magnetic Poles to nearly 0° at the Equator. It is measured by an inclinometer or dipometer, which is like a compass on its side. When pointed north–south, the inclinometer's magnetized needle swings to align itself with the Earth's lines of magnetic force as they enter the ground. For example, at Washington, DC, USA, the angle of dip is 71°. Small changes in both inclination and declination give clues to the kinds of rocks and minerals that might be underground.

Poles on the move

The Magnetic North and South Poles do not stay still. They 'wander' across the surface by up to several kilometres each year. These wandering poles do not affect most travellers. They do mean, however, that the Magnetic Poles must be tracked and measured year by year, so that very accurate maps can be updated.

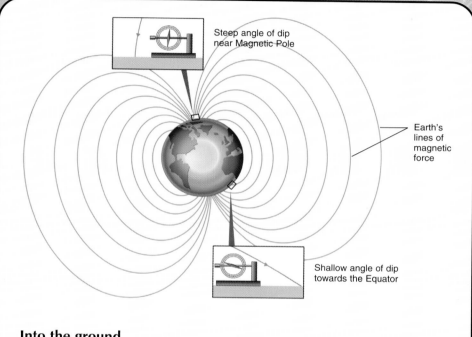

Steep angle of dip near Magnetic Pole

Earth's lines of magnetic force

Shallow angle of dip towards the Equator

Into the ground

The inclinometer or dipometer shows the angle at which the Earth's lines of magnetic force enter the ground. This varies around the planet's surface from the Magnetic North Pole to the Magnetic South Pole.

Flipping poles

In fact, at some point long ago, the Earth's whole magnetic field flipped or reversed. The Magnetic North Pole suddenly became the Magnetic South Pole, and vice versa. Exactly how this happened is not clear. But these magnetic reversals have occurred many times over millions of years. We may be heading for another flip in the future, perhaps a thousand years from now. Scientific measurements also show that the Earth's magnetic field is now less than half as strong as it was 10,000 years ago.

Magnetic skies

The air around us and the skies above are filled with various forms of magnetism, but most of them are invisible. They include the Earth's own magnetic field, which extends huge distances from the surface, up through the air of the atmosphere and out into space.

Animals and magnetism

Many creatures travel on long-distance journeys called migrations. Some probably use magnetism to help them find their way, as well as other navigating methods, such as the positions of the Sun, Moon and stars, and landmarks, such as mountains and rivers. These animals include many birds, from swifts and swallows to geese and swans, also great whales, sea turtles and fish, such as salmon and eels. These creatures may be able to sense the Earth's magnetic field, using tiny particles of iron-containing minerals in their bodies.

Built-in compass?
Animals, such as these migrating humpback whales, may have a natural sense of magnetism.

Magnetism in space

In the upper atmosphere more magnetism is made, in addition to the magnetic field from within the Earth. This is due to the solar wind – a continuous stream of various rays and fast-moving particles coming from the Sun. The solar wind hits the Earth's own magnetic field and the outer parts of the atmosphere at heights of more than 100 kilometres (60 miles) above the surface, and makes extra magnetic forces. These have only about 1/500th of the strength of the magnetic field from inside the Earth. The whole area of magnetism around the planet is called the magnetosphere. It is shaped not like a ball, but like a pear or teardrop. The blunt end faces the Sun and is about 50,000 kilometres (31,000 miles) above the Earth. The tapering end faces away from the Sun and is hundreds of times longer.

Storms and crackles

The magnetosphere is vast, far away and complicated, but it affects our daily lives in various ways. Magnetic storms occur when the solar wind changes, perhaps gaining strength for a time, and disturbs the Earth's magnetic field. Magnetic storms do not usually affect the ordinary weather of winds, clouds and rain. But they do affect radio waves and similar waves, which themselves are partly magnetic in nature. Such storms interfere with television and radio programmes, causing crackles and fuzzy pictures. They also affect radio and microwave signals going up and down to satellites. This can disrupt long-distance telephone calls and navigation by planes and ships. Magnetic storms may also cause surges of electricity in the long power lines that cross the countryside, perhaps leading to power cuts.

Magnetic lights

The *aurorae*, or northern and southern lights, are vast, shimmering, multi-coloured curtains of light that sometimes appear high in the night sky. They occur most often in the far north and south, near the Poles, at heights of between 50 and 300 kilometres (between 30 and 190 miles). They are made when the Earth's magnetic field 'grabs' rays and particles of the solar wind and pulls them towards its most powerful areas of magnetism near the Poles. The rays and particles collide with the Earth's own particles in the atmosphere and give out twinkles of light. The *aurora borealis* is seen in the far north, and the *aurora australis* in the far south.

Shining lights
The southern lights or aurora australis are due to tiny particles from the Sun colliding with Earth's magnetic forces.

Electrical magnets

A **permanent magnet**, such as an ordinary bar magnet, has magnetism which is present all the time. There is another kind of magnet, whose **magnetic field** can be turned on and off. This is the **electromagnet**. Its magnetic field works in exactly the same way as that of a permanent magnet, being most concentrated at the **poles**. And, as in a permanent magnet, like poles repel and unlike poles attract.

Sorting for recycling

An electromagnet, like a permanent magnet, attracts mainly iron-containing substances such as steels. In a scrapyard or recycling centre, it is important to sort out the steel and other iron-based metals called **ferrous metals**, from other metals, such as aluminium, brass and tin. An electromagnet can do this. As various metal objects pass by, the ferrous ones stick to the electromagnet. They are sent for recycling at the iron factory or steelworks. The aluminium and other metals carry on into different containers, since they have different methods of recycling.

Metal grab
Big magnets like this are used to lift, move and drop ferrous metals.

On and off

An electromagnet uses electricity to make magnetism. Whenever a flow of electricity, known as electric current, passes along a wire, this makes a magnetic field around the wire. It happens because electricity is the movement along the wire of the tiny parts of **atoms** called **electrons**. In a permanent magnet, the **magnetic force** comes from the spinning and orbits of electrons within their atoms.

In an electromagnet, the magnetic force also comes from moving electrons. But these electrons are jumping from one atom to the next, along the wire. The instant that the electricity flows, the magnetic field forms around the wire. And the instant electricity stops, the magnetic field disappears.

Wound into a coil

The magnetic field around a single straight wire is very weak. It can be made much stronger by curling the wire into a coil, called a **solenoid**. Coiling the wire brings together the magnetic fields around each turn of the coil, so they reinforce each other. The more coils, the stronger the magnetic field. Also the more powerful the electricity, measured as a higher **voltage**, the stronger the magnetic field.

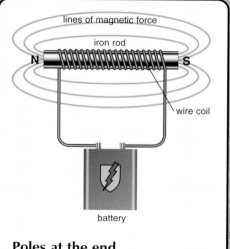

lines of magnetic force

iron rod

N   S

wire coil

battery

Poles at the end

The core of an electromagnet has lines of force, like those of a bar-shaped permanent magnet, with the most powerful magnetism at the ends.

The core in the middle

A further way to concentrate the magnetism is to put a rod of iron along the middle of the coil. This is called the **core** of the solenoid. The lines of magnetic force from the coil flow through the core and, by **magnetic induction**, make it work like a bar magnet. The core will attract magnetic items, repel the like pole of another magnet and attract its unlike pole – but only while the electricity flows. Making the electricity flow the other way through the coil reverses the magnetic poles of the core.

Electromagnets are used in hundreds of everyday machines and gadgets, as shown on the following pages.

Making electricity with magnets

When electricity flows through a wire as moving electrons, as explained on the previous page, a magnetic field is created around the wire. This is called the **electromagnetic effect**. The opposite is also true. When a magnetic field moves near a wire, electricity is made to flow through the wire. The moving magnetism affects the electrons in the wire and makes them jump or flow along, which creates the current. This principle is called **electromagnetic induction**. It is a vital part of the workings of thousands of machines, devices and gadgets.

Twang!

Most kinds of electric guitar rely on electromagnetic induction. The metal guitar strings pass over a magnetic pick-up, which contains a powerful bar magnet with a wire coil wound around it. When the string is plucked, it vibrates in the magnetic field of the bar magnet. This alters or distorts the field and moves its lines of **force** – which move in relation to the coil and so induce an electric current. A typical guitar magnetic pick-up has a coil with more than 10,000 turns – the wire is very, very thin!

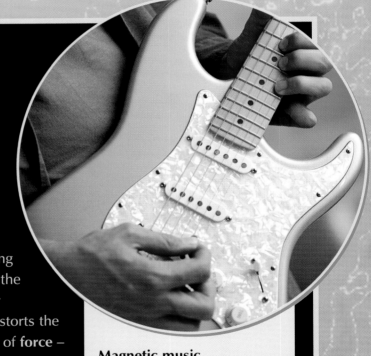

Magnetic music
The pick-ups under the strings on this electric guitar use magnetism to produce an electric current.

The need for change

In the electromagnetic effect, an electric current simply has to flow through a wire. There is no need for any movement of the wire or iron core. In electromagnetic induction, there is. If the magnet and wire stay still, then no electricity flows. There is a need for the magnet and the nearby wire to move in relation to each other. The wire can stay still as the magnet moves, or vice versa, or both can move. Like other features of magnetism and electricity, this can be explained in terms of electrons, which have their own tiny amounts of magnetism. As the magnetic field moves, it pushes the electrons along the wire, producing the electric current. If the magnet and the wire stay still in relation to each other, nothing happens.

Alternative change

An alternative to the magnet and wire moving in relation to each other, is the magnetic field changing strength. This is done using an electromagnet and feeding more or fewer **volts** through its coil. If the field becomes stronger or weaker, this induces a current to flow in a nearby wire, even if both the electromagnet and wire stay still.

Many uses

Electromagnetic induction is mentioned on many pages in this book, as part of the workings of microphones and motors. One of its main uses for daily life is in **generators** – machines that make electricity. In basic design, a generator has coils which are made to spin around in a magnetic field. This induces or generates electricity in the wires of the coils. The electricity supplied to our homes is produced in this way, by massive generators at power stations.

Magnetic wires in the road

Another common use of magnetism and electromagnetic induction is to control road traffic lights or signals. A series of wires is buried in the road, a few metres in front of the lights. The thin channels made for these can often be seen as zigzag marks across the road surface. A small electric current flows through the wire, making a magnetic field around it. As a vehicle passes over, its metal parts affect the field and alter the current, which is detected by the light control system. So the traffic lights 'know' if there are vehicles waiting.

Useful electromagnets

Electromagnets are made in all shapes and sizes, from smaller than the dot on this 'i' to bigger than a house. Some are powered by electricity from batteries, others use the higher voltage from the mains electricity supply. An advantage of the electromagnet, in addition to the fact that it can be switched on or off, is that it can be made much more powerful than a permanent magnet of the same size. This is done by having thousands of turns of wire in the coil, and by passing more volts of electricity through the wire. Some of the commonest big electromagnets are used in ironworks, steelyards and scrapyards. They can pick up girders of steel weighing many tonnes, or lift the steel-containing engine or body of a scrap car.

Sliding core

In some electromagnets the **core**, which is an iron bar, is fixed into the coil. In another design, the core is free to slide in and out of the coil. When the electricity is switched on, if the core is not in the middle of the coil, but poking out of one end, the coil's **magnetic field** pulls it powerfully into the middle. In this way, electricity is turned into magnetism, which is then turned into a sliding motion. This sliding-core **solenoid** is therefore said to turn electrical energy into mechanical energy or the energy of motion. The solenoid produces sliding-along or to-and-fro (reciprocating) motion. An electric motor does the same, but produces spinning or rotary movement.

Start the car

The sliding-core solenoid design is used in many everyday devices, from doorbells to cars. One of the most common uses is for starting a vehicle. When the key is turned, electricity is sent through a solenoid called the starter solenoid, near the engine. Fixed to the core of this solenoid is a heavy-duty electrical contact, designed for a large current. When the core slides along, with a small click, it turns on the heavy-duty electrical contact. This sends a huge current to the powerful electric motor, called the starter motor. This gets the engine turning so that it can start to run under its own power.

Unlock the car

The central locking system of a car uses four or five solenoids. To lock the doors, the car key switches on electricity to a solenoid inside each door. This pulls its core into it, and the core is attached to the locking mechanism, which slides along to work the door lock. To unlock, the electricity flows to another solenoid, next to the first one. This pulls the core back to slide the locking mechanism the other way.

Sliding magnets

In a car with central locking, turning the key switches on electricity to several solenoids, one in each door, which then work the locks.

Ding-dong

In a doorbell with 'ding-dong' chimes, pressing the doorbell button makes electricity flow through a solenoid, which pulls the sliding iron core into it. As this happens one end of the solenoid hits one chime to make the 'ding'. When the doorbell button is released, the electricity stops and the core is released. A spring pulls the core back out of the solenoid, and the core's other end hits the other chime to make the 'dong'.

A similar system is used for a remote-controlled door lock, as described in the panel on this page. This kind of 'flip-flop' or 'in-out' solenoid system is also used in many toys and games, such as radio-controlled cars and planes.

Sounds magnetic

Every time we listen to a radio or television, or to a music system, we hear sounds that are made with the help of magnets. This is because magnets are important parts of loudspeakers. Most loudspeakers use both permanent magnets and electromagnets.

Inside a speaker

Inside the cabinet or casing, the basic design of the speaker itself is a funnel shape called the cone or, sometimes, the **diaphragm**. This is the part which we can see from the front, as a round, dark cone behind the cover of cloth or metal grill. The cone has a coil of wire attached at the narrow end behind it.

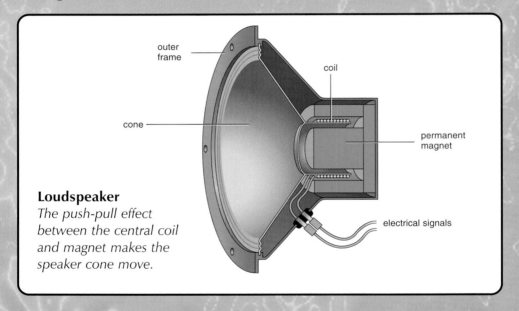

outer frame

coil

cone

permanent magnet

Loudspeaker
The push-pull effect between the central coil and magnet makes the speaker cone move.

electrical signals

This wire coil, sometimes called the voice coil, is wound on to a ring-shaped piece of thin card or plastic. The voice coil usually fits inside or into a round slot within a powerful permanent magnet. This permanent magnet is shaped like a ring or U, and is usually very heavy. In a typical speaker, almost half the total weight is due to the permanent magnet.

To and fro very fast

Wires bring electricity from the sound system to flow through the wire coil. As the electricity flows, it turns the coil into an electromagnet with its own magnetic field. This field attracts or repels the field of the permanent magnet, depending on which way the electricity flows.

The attracting and repelling forces pull and push the coil and make it move to and fro. The coil is attached to the cone, so the cone moves to and fro or vibrates as well. This happens hundreds or thousands of times each second. The vibrations of the cone produce sound waves, which travel out into the air.

Speaker in reverse

A loudspeaker changes electrical signals into sounds. A microphone does the reverse – and it works in the opposite way. In a moving-coil microphone, sound waves hit a thin, flexible sheet, or diaphragm, under the protective mesh. This sheet is the equivalent of the cone in the loudspeaker. A small coil of wire is attached to it, with a strong permanent magnet near by. As sound waves vibrate the diaphragm and coil, the coil moves in the field of the permanent magnet. This causes varying amounts of electricity to flow in the wire of the coil. The pulses of electricity produced are electrical copies of the sounds coming into the microphone.

Moving to the music

Vinyl discs are used by many club DJs (disc jockeys) for music events. The disc has sounds stored as patterns of tiny waves in a long groove in the record's surface. A stylus or needle runs along this groove and the waves make it vibrate. The stylus sticks out from a box-like part smaller than a thumb, called the pick-up. This works in a similar way to a microphone. Inside the pick-up, the other end of the stylus has tiny coils of wire fixed to it, and these coils are next to a permanent magnet. Vibrations of the stylus make the wire coils move in the magnetic field. This produces electrical signals in the wire coils, which are fed to the sound system.

Pick-up sounds
This DJ is 'scratching' – moving a record backwards and forwards – to achieve the sound he's looking for.

Looks magnetic

Without magnets and electromagnetism, we would have no television or computer screens. At least, we would not have the traditional types of screen, which are glass-fronted, quite heavy and often called tubes or cathode ray tubes (CRTs).

Testing a television
This engineer is watching two screens. The large one to the upper right is the television under test. The smaller one to the middle left is an oscilloscope, showing waves of electric current. Both screens use various combinations of electricity and magnetism.

Guns and screens

The basis of the CRT is a large glass container, which is nicknamed the tube, but is more usually shaped like a funnel. At the narrow end are parts called electron guns. These have very small metal wires or plates, which become very hot and send out electrons – the tiny parts of atoms that produce both magnetic fields and electric currents. The guns fire their electrons, billions every second, along the inside of the tube, to hit the inner surface of the far end, which is the screen.

On the screen, the electrons hit tiny dots of chemicals called phosphors, which coat the inside of the screen. When the dots are hit, they glow with light. We see this light from the other side of the clear glass screen as the television or computer image. In colour television, there are three colours of dots – red, green and blue.

Scanning

Where do magnets come in all this? Moving electrons make magnetism – and moving electrons can be affected by a magnetic field. In one design of television or computer screen, around the middle of the glass tube are sets of electromagnets, sometimes called focusing coils or deflector coils. Their magnetic fields affect the electrons whizzing past inside the tube and make them change direction or deflect, according to how the electromagnets switch on and how much electricity passes through them. In this way the beam of electrons from a gun can be made to angle up and down, and side to side.

The beam of electrons starts by hitting an upper corner of the screen. The electromagnets make the beam move in a line across the top of the screen, then do the same a tiny bit lower down the screen, and so on. This happens line by line, from side to side, all the way down the screen. This is called scanning.

Too fast to see

Scanning happens so fast that the whole screen is covered with hundreds of lines in less than one twentieth of a second. Our eyes cannot see the patterns of dots building up line by line. The pattern forms an image on the screen. This fades almost as soon as it forms. Then the same happens for the next picture on the screen, and so on, more than twenty pictures each second. Again, it all occurs so fast that our eyes merge the pictures together, and they seem to be moving.

Magnetic screen

In some television and computer screens, stray areas of magnetism and static electricity gradually build up on the glass tube and other parts. These can make the picture blurred and oddly coloured, and may also cause flickering and crackling. Some screens have a button to create a surge of magnetism that 'cleans' the stray areas, or this can happen automatically when the set is switched on or off. This is called degaussing.

Moving by magnetism

One of our most useful everyday machines uses magnetism – the electric **motor**. Early types of motor were devised in the 1830s by Michael Faraday and American physicist Joseph Henry. A typical house today may have more than a hundred of them. One type is used in small battery-powered devices, from electric toothbrushes to laptop computers. It is called the DC or **direct current** motor, because the battery that powers it makes an electric current that flows constantly in one direction.

DC motor

The DC motor has both **electromagnets** and **permanent magnets**. In the simplest design, the electromagnet is a coil of wire on a long rod, called the shaft, which can spin around. The coil is sometimes called the armature of the motor. It is placed between the two ends of a U-shaped permanent magnet.

Electricity passes through the coil of wire and turns it into an electromagnet. The direction of the electricity means that the north **pole** of the electromagnet is next to the north pole of the permanent magnet, and the south pole of the electromagnet is next to the permanent magnet's south pole. Like poles repel, and as they push away from each other they cause the coil to spin around half a turn on its shaft. This brings the north pole of the permanent magnet and the south pole of the electromagnet nearer, as they attract each other.

Switching poles

Electricity is fed to the coil through two parts called brushes. These press from either side on to a ring-shaped part on the shaft, the **commutator**.

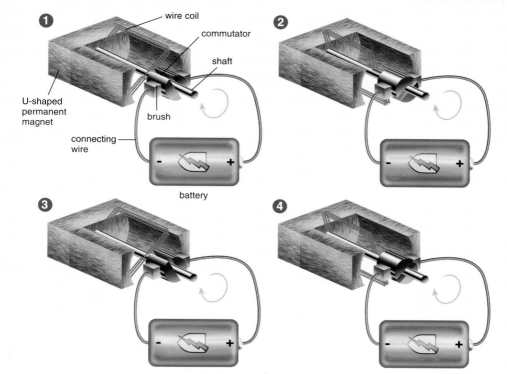

1 wire coil / commutator / shaft

U-shaped permanent magnet

brush

connecting wire

battery

2

3

4

DC motor

For each turn of a DC motor, the electric current is reversed by a 'rotating switch' called the commutator. This makes the coil into an electromagnet with poles that reverse as it turns. The push-pull interaction with the permanent magnet keeps the coil spinning.

The commutator is actually in two halves, each connected to an end of the wire that forms the coil. As the coil spins half a turn, the commutator does too, and as the half-rings move around each is pressed by the brush on the opposite side. This makes the electricity flow the other way through the coil, which reverses the coil's north and south poles. The permanent magnet stays the same. So again, like poles are near each other, and they repel. The shaft spins onwards – but after another half-turn, the commutator reverses the electricity again, and so on. In this way the spinning continues and the motor goes around.

Many pushes and pulls

In most real motors, there are several coils of wire on the shaft and the commutator is split into many segments. This means the magnetic attractions and repulsions happen many times for each turn of the motor, which gives a smoother and more powerful turning **force**.

More about motors

In a typical house there are motors in all kinds of appliances, from washing machines and freezers to electric screwdrivers and can-openers. They run on electricity from the mains supply. This is not direct current or DC, as is electricity from a battery. It is **alternating current** or AC, which means it changes or alternates its direction of flow, going one way and then the other, many times each second. Alternating current is used for mains electricity partly because it can drive a powerful type of electric motor called the **induction motor**, which direct current cannot do. The AC induction motor is usually quieter and more reliable because it does not have brushes and a commutator, which are the parts that wear out quickest in a DC motor. Other types of AC motors use brushes and bushes (slip-rings).

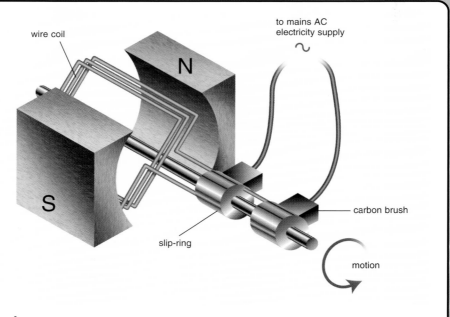

to mains AC electricity supply

wire coil

N

S

slip-ring

carbon brush

motion

Brush-type AC motor
The non-induction AC motor has pad-like brushes, similar to a DC motor. These press on collar-shaped slip-rings (bushes) to pass electricity to the coil. As the current flows one way then the other, the motor spins once.

Two sets of coils

The AC induction motor has a set of wire coils, which work as electromagnets, mounted on a shaft that can spin round. This part of the design is similar to that of the DC motor. But the AC induction motor does not have permanent magnets around the outside. Instead it has more wire coils, arranged in a ring. The inner set of coils, which can spin, is called the **rotor**. The outer set, which stays still, is known as the **stator**. To make the motor work, alternating current is fed through the coils of the stator, but not all at the same time. The electricity is timed so that it produces a **magnetic field** in each coil in turn, in very fast succession. The effect is that the magnetic field 'hops' from one coil to the next, so that it seems to go round and round the stator.

Magnetic speed

The first vehicles to hold the world land speed record, in the 1890s, were cars powered by electric motors. These electric cars reached speeds of up to 105 kilometres (65 miles) per hour. But from about 1900 petrol engines, and then jet engines, were used to power record-breaking cars. Today's land speed record for a car powered by an electric motor is 393 kilometres (244 miles) per hour. This is only one-third the speed of the fastest jet-powered cars.

Rotor and stator

The coils of the rotor do not receive electricity along wires. But as the magnetic field goes round and round the stator, this makes electricity flow in the coils of the rotor, by induction. This electricity turns the coils of the rotor into electromagnets, and they attract or repel the magnetic field of the stator. The movement of the stator's magnetic field is carefully timed so that it 'drags' the rotor with it, and so the rotor spins around.

DC and AC motors are called electric motors. But magnetism is equally important. A better name might be magnetic-electric motors, or perhaps electric-magnetic motors. Although modern motors are very reliable, they do sometimes break down or wear out. The problem often begins with the machinery attached to the motor. This becomes worn or stiff, so the motor has to produce more turning force to make the machinery work. As the strain on the motor increases, it has to turn more slowly and with greater force. More magnetism is needed to do this, which means that more electric current flows through the wire coils. More current and slower rotation makes heat build up in the coils. Eventually the motor burns out.

Micro-magnetism

Magnetism can be used to push, pull, slide, spin, lift, turn – and store. Writing is a way of storing information as marks on paper. In the same way, information can be 'written' as patches of magnetism in a magnetic substance, known as the **magnetic medium**. The patches of magnetism cannot be seen because they are far too small, and in any case magnetism is not visible. Besides this, they do not make shapes like letters and words on paper. The patterns of magnetism are more like lines or dots with spaces between, as a code for the information. However, the principle is similar to that of writing. Keeping information this way is known as magnetic data storage. It is likely that you use it every day, often without thinking, as we will see later in this book.

Write

How is information 'written' on to a magnetic medium and then 'read' again for use? The key part is the read-write head. One basic design for this is a tiny U-shaped piece of metal called a yoke, with wire coils around it. If electricity flows through the coils for a tiny fraction of a second, they turn the yoke into an **electromagnet**.

The **magnetic field** across the gap of the yoke is very near the surface of the magnetic medium. The field affects the tiny magnetic particles of the medium and makes them 'flip' to form a patch of magnetism, like giving many tiny bar magnets a certain direction or alignment.

Small head
The tiny read-write head of a computer magnetic hard disc is at the narrow end of the swinging arm, to the lower left of the picture. It rests on the disc's surface layer of magnetic particles.

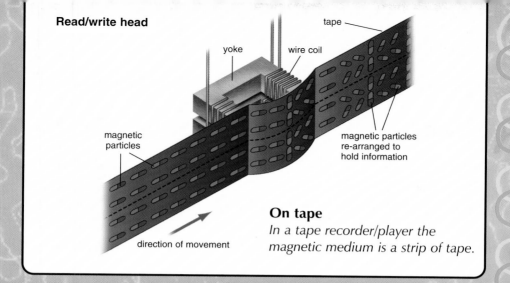

Read/write head

yoke

wire coil

tape

magnetic particles

magnetic particles re-arranged to hold information

direction of movement

On tape
In a tape recorder/player the magnetic medium is a strip of tape.

During this time, the magnetic medium is moving past the read-write head. So the head 'writes' a tiny patch of magnetism on it, then another one slightly farther along, and so on. Information consists of millions of these tiny patches 'written' as the medium moves past the head.

Read

To obtain stored information, the medium again moves past the read-write head. As a patch of magnetism goes past, it produces a tiny electrical current in the wire coils, by **electromagnetic induction**. So as the medium moves, the head detects the patterns and spaces of the patches, and feeds the electrical signals to other parts of the machine.

The smaller the patches of magnetism, the more information can be stored in an area. Similarly, the faster the medium moves past the head, the more patches can be stored per second, so the total amount of information is greater. In some designs the read and write heads are two separate devices.

So much information

Engineers are gradually packing more and more information on to magnetic storage media. At present, tens of billions of patches can be stored in an area smaller than a fingernail. If you tried to write these patches as zeroes like this '0', on paper, you would need a piece of paper two kilometres by one kilometre. Engineers hope one day to be able to store all the information for the pictures and sounds of a full-length movie on a patch of magnetic medium the size of this '0'.

Magnetic media

There are many kinds of magnetic media for storing information in coded form, as tiny spots or stripes of magnetism. They include audio cassette tapes, DAT (**digital audio tapes**), video cassette tapes, various kinds of magnetic computer discs, such as floppy discs and hard discs, and the strips or stripes on identity cards, bank cards and similar items. (CDs and DVDs work using light rather than magnetism.)

Most of these magnetic media have the same basic structure. There is a base layer, which for a tape is a type of flexible plastic, but for a disc is stiffer. On this is a magnetic layer, which contains billions of tiny grains of **magnetic material**. On the top is the shiny surface layer, which both protects the magnetic layer underneath and allows the read-write head to skim across without wear or scratching.

Tapes and discs

One problem with magnetic tape of any kind is that it must be wound along past the read-write head. So finding a particular piece of information at the end of the tape, if the tape is positioned near the beginning, takes time as the tape winds along. Another problem is known as print-through. When a tape is wound on to its spool or reel, the spiral windings of the tape press against each other. The tiny patches of magnetism in one winding of the tape are very close to the patches of the windings on either side of it. If the tape is not used for a long period, and stays tightly wound, the patches on adjacent windings can disturb and distort each other.

In all forms of magnetic storage, a powerful magnetic field nearby can destroy the stored information by disrupting the magnetic patches. Sources of powerful magnetic fields include the **permanent magnets** of loudspeakers and the electromagnetic coils of **motors** and television sets. Leaving a magnetic tape or disc next to these can destroy the information. So can excessive heat or physical knocks and vibrations – just as in an ordinary bar magnet.

A magnetic disc gets around the lengthy problem of winding. The read-write head is on an arm and can swing from the outside of the disc across to its centre, like the magnetic pick-up for a vinyl disc record deck. At the same time, the disc spins 100 or more times each second. With the swinging arm and spinning disc, the information on a particular part of the disc can be reached in a few thousandths of a second. In a computer hard drive, there is usually not one disc, but a stack of ten or more, each five to ten centimetres across, with a space above each one for a swinging arm with its own read-write head. The head is positioned just 20 millionths of one millimetre from the surface of its disc. At such tiny distances, a speck of dust would seem like a huge boulder. So computer hard drives are sealed inside airtight boxes to keep dust out.

Swipe-read

The magnetic strips on security and bank cards also use tiny patches of magnetism. These are read by a swipe machine. The card's magnetic strip moves past a read head, which detects the magnetism by electromagnetic induction.

Magnetic 'key'
Some locked doors are opened by cards rather than keys. The card's magnetic code works a **solenoid** *to undo the lock.*

Electromagnetic waves

We have seen how electromagnetism is a vital part of everyday devices. It is also all around us as different kinds of waves and rays.

Carrying information

Electromagnetic waves include radio waves, which carry information to our radios, broadcast (non-cable) television channels and mobile phones. Radio waves are also sent up to satellites in space, which beam them back down to different areas on Earth. They are also used in radar systems, which beam out pulses of radio waves and then detect and analyze the 'echoes' which bounce off objects around. Radar is used by planes, ships, weather satellites and in many other important ways.

Waves from space
Normal or optical telescopes see light from space. Radio telescopes detect radio waves from space. They are dish-shaped, like the dishes which receive satellite radio signals.

Two waves in one

It is difficult to picture an electromagnetic wave. It can be thought of as not one typical up-and-down, wavy-line-type wave, but two. One of these contains magnetic **energy**. The other wave is at right angles to the first and contains the electrical energy. Each kind of wave has an equal amount of energy, which is indicated by the height of its peak or the depth of its trough. Both the magnetic and the electrical waves build to an upper peak at the same time, then fade away to zero, fall to their troughs, and rise again to zero – all the time staying in step with each other.

Electromagnetic waves travel incredibly fast, at the speed of light, which is about 300,000 kilometres (186,300 miles) per second. Light is one type of electromagnetic wave.

The electromagnetic spectrum

There are many other kinds of electromagnetic wave, in addition to radio. They form a whole range or spectrum, also known as electromagnetic radiation. They include:

- Microwaves, which are used not only for cooking but also for carrying information, in the same way as radio waves. They are sent between tall towers and beamed up and down to satellites in space.
- Infra-red waves or rays, which carry heat energy. The warmth of the Sun is due to its infra-red waves travelling to us through space.
- Light rays, which we detect with our eyes.
- Ultra-violet waves. Like light and infra-red, these also come from the Sun. UV can burn and damage the skin.
- X-rays, used in medicine to see inside the body, and also for many scientific purposes.
- Gamma rays, which are used on certain kinds of food and other objects to sterilize them (kill all the germs).

How long are the waves?

In the range or spectrum of electromagnetic waves, radio waves are the longest. Their wavelengths vary from several kilometres to less than a metre. Microwaves are mostly between 1000 and 10 millimetres long. Next shortest are infra-red waves, with hundreds in one millimetre. Then come light waves, with wavelengths of less than one-thousandth of a millimetre. Even shorter are ultra-violet waves, and then X-rays. Shortest of all are gamma rays, where a million million waves joined together would only stretch one millimetre.

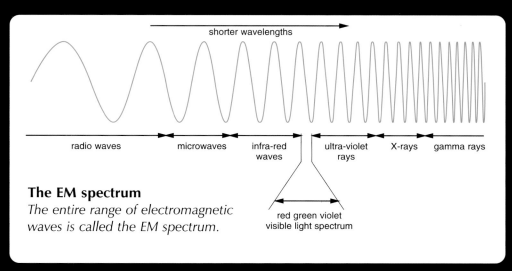

shorter wavelengths

radio waves | microwaves | infra-red waves | ultra-violet rays | X-rays | gamma rays

red green violet
visible light spectrum

The EM spectrum
The entire range of electromagnetic waves is called the EM spectrum.

Magnetic medicine

Magnetism is used in health and medicine in several ways. X-rays are incredibly short electromagnetic waves, which can pass through softer parts of the body, such as muscles and blood vessels. But they cannot pass through harder, denser parts, especially bones. So X-ray images are used to check for broken bones and for other health problems, such as certain kinds of growth or tumour. However, too much exposure to X-rays can damage the body, so these ordinary or plain X-rays are used carefully and in a very limited way.

CT scans

Another way to see inside the body using X-rays is with a CT or computerized tomography scanner (also called CAT, computerized axial tomography). This uses very weak and harmless X-rays, which are beamed through the body at different angles and positions and sensed by detectors on the other side. A computer analyzes the results and builds up a picture of the body's internal parts, including soft ones such as blood vessels and nerves.

MR scans

MR or magnetic resonance scanning (also called MRI, magnetic resonance imaging) is another form of diagnostic imaging – making a picture of what is happening inside the body, to identify or diagnose a problem. A person is placed in a large tunnel-like scanner that contains huge sets of ring-shaped electromagnets.

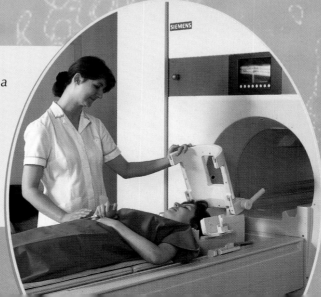

MR scanner
This person is about to enter a magnetic resonance scanner. The ring-shaped magnets are inside the machine's casing, and their holes form a 'tunnel' where the person lies on a sliding bed.

These produce a very powerful magnetic field, almost 100,000 times stronger than Earth's natural magnetism. The field is so strong that all objects that could be magnetic must be kept well away, or they could be attracted from some distance and 'fly' through the air to stick to the machine. Such objects include jewellery worn by the patient or the scanner operators. If an MR magnet attracted a metal belt buckle, it would be very difficult to pull the buckle away again.

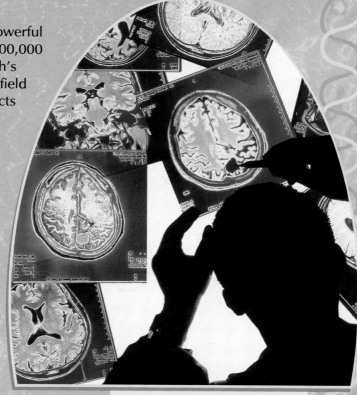

Magnetic diagnosis
A doctor examines MR scans of the brain on a backlit screen, to identify or diagnose any illness.

The intense magnetism of the scanner affects many of the **atoms** in the body and causes them to line up, like billions of tiny magnetic compass needles. Then a pulse of radio waves is fired into the body as the magnetic field is changed. The lined-up atoms respond by wobbling out of line, which makes them give off their own tiny radio pulses. Detectors in the machine receive these and they are analyzed by computer to build up a very detailed picture of internal body parts.

Is magnetism harmful?

We live constantly in the Earth's magnetic field. However there are worries that stronger magnetism may cause harm. Several scientific studies have tried to find out if electromagnetic waves – for example, the radio waves to and from a mobile phone – might affect the brain. There is no clear evidence as yet. But in case there is a link, many people prefer to use hands-free mobile phone equipment or send text messages, rather than holding the mobile phone near to their ear and brain.

Odd magnetism and supermagnets

The form of magnetism described so far in this book is called ferromagnetism, because it is based on the metal iron (which has the scientific symbol Fe, short for the Latin word *ferrum*, meaning iron). This is not the only form of magnetism, however. There are other forms that scientists are studying, and which may become useful in the future.

More forms of magnetism

In diamagnetism, a substance exposed to a nearby magnetic field gains its own magnetism. But this magnetism repels it from a magnetic field. The metal bismuth shows this feature. This is the opposite of ferromagnetism, where the **force** is attraction. In paramagnetism, a substance that is not ferromagnetic is given magnetism by a nearby magnetic field, and is attracted to the strongest part of that field. Two strongly paramagnetic substances are the rare metals platinum and palladium.

Ultra-power magnets

Very powerful and specialized magnets are used in many kinds of scientific research, and some of these ideas could be used in everyday life in the future. Almost any substance can be made to respond to magnetism of some kind – even a frog! In one experiment, a frog was subjected to such a powerful magnetic field that it became a magnet itself, and it was made to float by magnetic repulsion.

This type of scientific research may well sound strange, but it might lead to undreamed-of uses for magnetism.

Famous frog!
This frog has been magnetized and is floating as a result of a form of maglev called magnetic repulsion; it may be a bit surprised, but was not hurt!

In nuclear power stations, electricity is made from the energy released when the centres of atoms split apart. This process is called **nuclear fission**. However, the process produces dangerous radioactivity. An alternative may be **nuclear fusion**, where parts of atoms are joined together. This would produce much less radioactivity. However, to make fusion happen temperatures of 100 million °C are needed – far hotter than the Sun. No physical object can touch a substance at this temperature. It can only be contained by incredibly powerful magnetic fields from electromagnets. Scientists continue to study fusion power as a source of energy for the future.

Magnets in the future

One area of active research at the moment is into producing superconductor materials for wires, which could carry electricity much more effectively than the materials used for this today. This would allow electromagnets to make much more powerful magnetic fields, and would save vast amounts of energy and natural resources. In medicine, new techniques might use magnetism from superconductor electromagnets to heal disease and relieve pain. It would also make **maglev** trains (see page 16) need much less electricity for their electromagnets.

The maglev idea might even be adapted to launch spacecraft! The craft would gain speed very rapidly by racing along a track powered by a line of superconducting electromagnets. It could be 'fired' into space, almost like a bullet from a gun. One day there may even be anti-gravity devices that use magnetism, such as cars without wheels that float above the ground, or even a suit that is worn on the body so a person can fly.

Superconductor
Superconductors carry electricity almost perfectly, far better than ordinary wires. Their magnetic fields easily make small objects levitate or 'float'.

The science of magnetism can be very complicated. It involves words that are unfamiliar to most of us, such as **magnetic flux**, **domains**, **solenoids** and **electron** spin. There are many features and processes to remember – not only the simple rule that 'like magnetic **poles** repel; unlike poles attract', but also ideas such as **electromagnetic induction** and the **electromagnetic effect**. Even expert scientists have difficulty in explaining some of the more detailed aspects of **magnetic fields** and **magnetic forces**. Also magnetism itself is invisible. Often it is difficult to understand what we cannot see.

The units that measure magnetism are also unfamiliar. We become familiar with units such as metres for length and grams for weight, when we can see what we are measuring. Magnetic units such as **teslas** and **webers** are much more difficult to appreciate, especially as we cannot see the magnetism they are measuring. Yet these units are vitally important to designers and engineers in many areas of science and technology, from radio communications to power stations.

Magnets on the Moon
When astronauts landed on the Moon, from 1969 to 1972, they took with them experiments to study magnetism in space and on other worlds.

Yet magnets and magnetism are all around us – from the Earth's magnetic field, to the hundreds of magnets and **electromagnets** we use in everyday life. When we switch on any machine powered by an electric **motor**, turn on the television, listen to music from a sound system or radio, use a vehicle central locking system or click a cupboard door closed by its magnetic catch, we are using magnetism. Often the magnetism is combined with its twin, electricity, as **electromagnetic force** – one of the most important **forces** in the whole Universe.

Glossary

alternating current (AC) flow of electricity that changes direction, usually many times per second

atom tiniest particle of a pure substance, which is itself made up of smaller or subatomic particles

commutator part of an electric motor that reverses the direction of electrical flow to the wire coils as the motor spins

core in an electromagnet, the bar or rod (usually iron) placed in the solenoid (coil of wire)

declination difference in angle between the direction a compass needle points to, and true magnetic north where it should point

diaphragm thin sheet that can vibrate easily, used in microphones and loudspeakers

digital working in small separate steps or stages

direct current (DC) flow of electricity in one direction only

domains tiny areas of magnetism that make up a larger magnet

electric charge a type of force, either positive or negative, possessed by particles in an atom, especially protons (+) and electrons (–)

electromagnet device that produces magnetism from flowing electricity, where the magnetism disappears when the electricity is switched off

electromagnetic effect producing magnetism using electricity

electromagnetic force combined electrical and magnetic energy

electromagnetic induction producing electricity using magnetism

electrons subatomic particles with a negative charge

ferrous metal metallic substance made of or containing iron

force push or pull which causes a change in movement or shape

generator device that changes movement energy into electricity

hard in magnetism, a substance made into a magnet that keeps its magnetism for a long time

inclination angle at which Earth's invisible lines of magnetic force enter the ground

induction motor motor that uses alternating current (AC)

maglev magnetic levitation, the use of magnetism to lift (levitate) or move objects

magnetic field area around a magnet where the magnetic effect extends

magnetic flux broadly, strength or amount of magnetism

magnetic force push or pull exerted on magnetic material by a magnet

magnetic induction production by a magnet of another magnetic field in an object near by

magnetic medium substance that retains tiny patches of magnetism and is used to store information in magnetic form

motor usual name for electric motor, which turns electricity into the energy of movement using magnetic forces

neutron subatomic particle with no charge, found in the nucleus of an atom

nuclear fission reaction in which the nucleus of an atom splits into various parts, releasing energy

nuclear fusion reaction in which two small, light nuclei fuse together to form a single heavier nucleus, releasing energy

nucleus central part of an atom, containing protons and neutrons

permanent magnet magnet that retains its magnetic force all the time

pole in magnetism, one of the two places on a magnet where the magnetic force is strongest

proton positively charged subatomic particle found in the nucleus of an atom

retentivity ability of a substance to retain its magnetic field over a long period

rotor in a generator or electric motor, a coil of wire or group of coils that rotate

soft in magnetism, a substance made into a magnet by another magnetic field that loses its magnetism when the other field is removed

solenoid wire wound into a long coil, as used in electromagnets

static electricity electrical charge that builds up on an object as electrons are either rubbed off or deposited on to it

stator in a generator or electric motor, a coil of wire or group of coils that stay still and do not rotate

subatomic particles particles smaller than an atom, such as the electrons, protons and neutrons which make up atoms

tesla unit of magnetic flux density, used to measure the amount of magnetism (magnetic flux) in a certain area, 1 tesla = 1 weber per square metre (see **weber**)

transformer device which changes the voltage in an electrical system

volt unit for measuring the strength or push of electricity (potential difference)

voltage the strength or push of electricity (potential difference)

weber unit of magnetic flux or amount of magnetism, for example, used to measure the strength of the whole magnetic field around a magnet (see **tesla**)